LOVE AND GRIEF
IN THE
TIME OF KETU

PIANTA

Cover design: Pianta
Cover photograph, Monicore, Pixabay.

ACKNOWLEDGMENTS

Much appreciation to family and friends for all of their love, patience, and good humor. A special thank you to David Hawthorne for his depth of knowledge and kindness with which he shares his gifts. Many thanks to Erika, Babak, Chase, and Anna for their talents and the time spent workshopping. Much appreciation also to Erika for her insights, spirit, artistry and wit–and to Delaina Thomas, who saw poems in some of my emails years ago, some of which appear here. And as always, deep gratitude for the loving influence of Kumu Kapena and Kumu Lokelani, who continue to bring grace and joy to everyone around them.

INTRODUCTION

These poems reflect a very spiritual time for me. I refer to it as the "time of Ketu" because, although I have very limited knowledge of the planets and their influences, what little I did know gave me a way to understand what I was experiencing. This way of looking at things also reassured me that there are remedies for everything and that are many kinds of beauty, no matter what the circumstances are.

TABLE OF CONTENTS

UNDER THE INFLUENCE OF KETU 14

I UNDERSTAND NOW 16

CHANGE OR BE CHANGED 18

NONVIOLENCE AND WILL 20

DREAMS 22

BORN IN KETU 24

HERE 26

THE MAN WITH THE BIRTHDAY CAKE 29

LENIENCY 30

TODAY IS THE DAY 32

ALL THINGS BEING EQUAL 34

ALLOWANCE 36

PART OF ME 40

TO THE 108 NAMES OF SHIVA 42

AT THIS MOMENT 44

EVERYONE WANTS TO SLEEP 46

I CAN WRITE THIS POEM 48

HONEST EGO 50

IN THIS WORLD 52

TAKE THE PRESSURE OFF 56

THE ESSENTIAL NATURE OF THINGS 58

I'D LIKE TO KNOW 59

NOT WHAT IT SEEMS 60

CARING 61

ON THE WAY TO REAL 62

COMPANIONS 64

SOMEONE TOLD ME 66

UNDER THE INFLUENCE OF KETU

I am under the influence
of Ketu

and no physical comforts
can be found here

it is a bare house
clean
and quiet

and I am without
adornment

everything extraneous
has been shattered away
or torn by wind

if anything can grow here
will it be love?

will it be
for all men, women, and children
for all creatures that roam the earth
and for all that is avian above them
whether small or daunting
or as finite

as the beating of ladybug wings?

in a year when everything false fails
I face the Creator
and all that I hold
is cracked away

and all that I am
can spill out
as viscous
as the morning sun
with nothing left to shield me

under the influence of Ketu
I am humbled
waiting for what draws near

I UNDERSTAND NOW

I understand now
why shrines are built
and garlands laid
why thousands line the streets
bodies overheated
under the weight of thick marigolds
threaded on string
everyone pressed together to feel the mass
of vulnerability
the spirit held within the flesh
why millions bow down
and wash in the Ganges

why the colors of the 9 Grahas
light everything everywhere
Lakshmi
and Shiva
radiate from every bit
and corner
and chants and offerings
circulate in the air

why scriptures proclaim
the blinding *Light of God*

it irons flat

any wavering we feel
and everything is seen
through a kaleidoscope
the multiplicity of matrices
dividing into action and reaction
as the significations of houses and planets
nearly careen or collide

they overshadow each other
in loops of polarities
and bounce against orbits
like yo-yos on a taut string

why it all comes down to timing
and prostrations on the floor

from which visions rise up
like heat
in veils of benevolences
or redemptive strikes
all things being equal

we feel everything

having surrendered to the laws of the body
having gazed into the eyes of the Lord

CHANGE OR BE CHANGED

that phrase keeps appearing
in my head

my recalcitrance
seared off of me
like the controlled burns
before fire season

> *Some seeds, such as sequoia, remain dormant until fire*
> *breaks down the seed coating.*

they break free
to finally be planted
or roasted forever
off the face of the earth

in such extremes
I need the strength of Mars—
Mangal—
appeased by the wavelengths of red coral

so that when I start to feel what is coming
I won't struggle with the sense of unraveling
like the tabla that starts to gain speed
from eighths to sixteenths or more

I'll know that all of what this is
is what needs to be uncoiled and sprung

NONVIOLENCE AND WILL

I want to stop talking

words have been
spilling out of me for days

I want to retract them all
like a great drawing in of breath
but that will have no corresponding exhalation

instead I'd like to settle
as simple as a dog
circling in its bed
or like the final chattering
before the birds cease activity
at the start of night

I want to go inward as far as I can go

the final ahimsa
soaked through every fiber and cell
drenched
saturated

as heavy as bog
as thick as super-cooled liquid
alive yet viscous

just before it becomes brittle
before it can be shattercd
as utterly transparent glass

someday
I'd love to close up
the way sleeping grass does
nyctinastic
sensing movement
closing in darkness
opening in light

love spilling outward
without sound
without shards
eyes open
voiceless   solitary   bright

DREAMS

my dreams differ

the desire to go inward
so deep

like the barely seen ridge
of the blue whales–the Rorquals
that have shades of gray
but turn bright and luminous
submerged beneath the wave

beneath that
sinking further

where things barely move
the amorphous
poised on the membrane of not yet manifest

till then
I remain restless
like a giant body
from Mesozoic times
one of the ungainly
land bound
that travels
as the four footed

blinking
unable to escape
the linear and unceasing
confinements of day/night/day/night
caught stranded in this world

attempting to cross
the breach

BORN IN KETU

You were born in the last seven months of a seven-year
cycle ruled by Ketu. Ketu is the root of your tree of life.
David Hawthorne, M.S., J.B.

born into this
I am at home
with renunciation

the gift of taking away

familiar with deficits
that awaken abundance

I feel steady
on a boat that's rocking to toss me free

I calm myself
along with the impulses to cut off
all worldly life

this too is Ketu
to strike the bell
and have all dust fly off

I want to control impending beasts
control the burns

excoriate
and atone
before being asked
in hopes of gaining favor

but I am not diverting the beasts
I am not controlling the burns

so I collect myself
and ask whatever
or whoever
is earnest
to protect me

I turn only to the vast cover of sky
and feel my heart beating furiously
anticipating the announcement of the onslaught
of sudden, deafening rain

HERE

claim the ground you walk on

as if the path were birthed for you
as sure as the way jasmine climbs
tendrils seeking up and around the wires
of fences
meant to hold others in
or others out

claim the ground
as sure as the rich earth
delivers spring
the v of trowels angling themselves
to pierce the boundaries of soil
the organic material
melding onto itself

> "Each shovel of soil holds more living things than all the
> human beings ever born."
> *The Dirt on Soil*

the dissolving of the self
that you always felt was on the verge of happening
didn't
so you've kept your bodily form
and you're here now

still resisting the laws of physics, of biological matter, of space

all of which are immutable

it starts to feel like a science of chains
that binds you here

but instead
claim the ground
claim the ground
claim the ground that you walk on

as if you were loved
as if you belonged
as if you were formed

to be born on this earth
to grow fully strong
and free

THE MAN WITH THE BIRTHDAY CAKE

the man with the birthday cake is happy
going through the line at Vons
the long pink sheet cake box
is declarative

the next in line comments
"someone's going to enjoy that"

"two-year old and three-year old, so I don't know
how much they're going to know"
he says
then asks the cashier for help with the discount card
and tape
to keep the box tightly closed

I feel consoled as he leaves
watching him lift it
like forklift and pallet
the cake secured
absolutely
reminded that life is rock solid
in the arms of someone
who loves

LENIENCY

leniency is narrow
like the gymnast's
wooden balance beam

falling is frequent
and no points are given

starting from that position
one can only leap again

wavering for a moment
you still need to dismount

with a hyper extended flourish
of arms and back

like a bird straining its chest
to lock in both feet

in order to land
and stand

TODAY IS THE DAY

for the vet who crashed
in a car two years after the war
and who goes to the wrong room
for our conference

for the one whose nephews were abducted
who checks his email fifty times a day
to see if he can find where they are
who hears months later
that one has been released
and then a month after that
the other has been freed
but now has a broken back
from torture

for the one who thanks me
and apologizes in his email *I'm responsible for failing
not you*
and for the one who argues against grade point averages
and their numerical conclusions

and this is the day for me
the one who is bereft
after her beloved brother's death

because the papers keep coming

and stacks keep rising
and I turn out work
like a Heidelberg press
churning, churning,
revolving,
burning
till my face, body
and soul
are a blur

ALL THINGS BEING EQUAL

it's hard to find anything
egalitarian
like servings for a dinner party–
wanting portions to be similarly fashioned–
hunting through the potato bin
for sizes that match

it is asymmetry

the ungoverned nature
of the uneven branch
that rises starkly against a matte sky

I pause before sorting the rooted vegetables
unsure if sameness is a kind of poverty
and transcendence of that
divine

ALLOWANCE

I cannot be consoled
I allow myself to say that this one day

I cannot be consoled
for he cannot return
in the form I can recognize
so he has returned to the embrace
of God, his true Father and Mother Divine

which all people say in their own way
and I say it too
but it feels delusional
because this grief is so deep
and so inevitable
that there is no such buffer that can be built

like the Greeks
whose women begin and end their widowhood
in black
stark against the bright white glare
of limestone
and blue, blue water

they know their place has changed
unalterably
so they reconfigure themselves

to live their lives
exiled

this is my moment to face my ignorance
utterly blind–
like all others who are blind

I rebel
I grieve

I grieve
till all the bones in me
break

he won't be coming back
not in the form I know
and everything I see
from leaf to stone
tree to flower
cries out a remembrance

I cannot be consoled

so I ask his forgiveness
and love him so much
that I cannot bear to see him delayed

so I let him

I let him

I let him

go

PART OF ME

part of me has died with you

no words for that
no less than that

in honor of you
I give that part
back to the universe
as if the loss of it
is a good thing
to be bestowed elsewhere

the gift that it was
now free
to be held by someone else

it was mine
so briefly

like petals
that pale
and
change
to meet some other
fate

awarded to some other soul
who'll find it and make sense of it
just as you encouraged what you found
and loved
in me

TO THE 108 NAMES OF SHIVA

I woke this morning
and realized why people
like tattoos
they want to have
a serpent wrapped around their waist
and bands of ink like bracelets painted around their arms
wrists and forearms
and to sit in lotus or half lotus
one leg with foot relaxed yet flexed
the foot of the arch curved
their fingers peaked
like head feathers of birds
vivacious in color
while the Dhurga sukhtam
plays with rings of its own
permanence
impermanence
intent
yet goal free

this is how I awoke
this morning
quiescent
alert
cognizant of the permanence of life
on the impermanence
of skin

AT THIS MOMENT

at this moment
our souls are alive

we are a part of this hum on this earth
our bodies corporeal and not merely atmospheric

we are not ethereal

the cheesecake Chase carried in a stiff cardboard box
sits as round as sundial
beneath the fluorescent light
and we eat it fully

we drift

we have conversations

the poems we read shift and take different shapes
as we expand or reduce a line here or there

on the outside we seem like flesh and bones
but on the inside
fractures of my splintered heart
soften, gel, coalesce,
meld back into a self I recognize

as I drive back in the dark night
I am flying–
being alive is suddenly lucky, good, and free

EVERYONE WANTS TO SLEEP

everyone wants to sleep

but no one sleeps

dimly lit rooms
beep with blue lights
or cell phones that ping
with messages

insomnia
hovers above us all
circling

what seeps in
and seeps out of us
is loneliness

we each get rationed a share

no one is spared
these moments

packed on trains
or alone at a table

a woman laying a napkin on her lap

or a man putting a violin in its case

melancholy pursues us

sleep evades

companionship has a taste
sharp and decisive
when a loved one
walks in

I CAN WRITE THIS POEM

I can write this poem
but I can't find a better place to live
I hear Sanskrit on the subtle
but my yard is full of weeds
I'm practically dressing in sweatpants at school
I look a mess
end-of-semester blues
worn out from surly aggressive students
unhappy with their grades
I'm partially comatose with grateful ones
who cry openly when they know they've passed

a friend gave me peonies
at a belated birthday lunch yesterday
they are huge and pink
the world is so full of angry people
even a "hello" can set someone off!

if I treated others the way I've been treated
no one would want to give me peonies
but here they recline
on my desk so beautiful
crepe-paper petal cups
curved so deep

HONEST EGO

coming back to the Self
that is my compass

sometimes I aspire to be humble
in order not to feed the ego
but if fear of criticism is mingled there
then I am protecting the ego

it may be that I know the ego
is on its way out
so ironically
or subconsciously I protect what's left
which actually sustains the ego
delaying evolution

what can be more devastating to an ego
than being trounced publicly

or is the greater test
adulation
how would I ever remain even keeled
without increasing the ego

maybe either case can roast the ego
to its final end

not a big ego or a small ego
but an honest ego

what other people do doesn't matter
I want to feel honest to myself
to know I did all that I could
with what I was given

IN THIS WORLD

weather is strange here
every day swirling events
shifting from cold to sunny
each of us a mystery unto ourselves

we have contracts but sometimes
good things happen to bad people
and bad things happen to good people
there's karma so fixed so exact
but also gaps
anomalies or things that have gone wrong
in terms of degrees
or the failure of those responsible for good
to step in

responses are fragile and complicated
no one should feel sure ruminating
we have all been injured parties
in this life or another
each of us has a right to feel what we feel
and to work it out
in our own way and time

sometimes people bury things they can't deal with
or try to bury people who bring them up
I support anyone who has the guts

to try to face these things
it's hard
it takes courage
that's love

I said no to a lot of opportunities
because I was afraid
I've gotten better at not losing who I am
to maintain the truth of myself

I come out of silence
I go back to silence
relationships and generations interweave
layers upon layers revolve
compete recede emerge
the magnitude of the moment
holds the grandeur of life
its peril as well
the innocence the wonder

the invincibility of the soul
ascends and transcends
like a bird circling round
returning to itself

tasks abound on the horizon

I feel the urgency of time
but I still find my way to the ocean
that bright blue piece of glass
holding in the yellow
heat
it turns into
photosynthesis green

TAKE THE PRESSURE OFF

three men in unity consciousness
may not be friends

take the pressure off trying to determine
who or what is absolutely right

choices may be different to different people
even with equal consciousness

sometimes being upfront works
like no, no, no--I'm a fish, you're a bird--
we've all got to follow our own nature

you burst out laughing and then it feels liberating
when two seconds earlier you felt
like a prisoner in your own environment

we don't realize we have the right to be as we are
we think it's about them liking us in the ways they are
but we are free to be a fish or a bird
it makes it a lot easier to be cordial

don't think about being bigger or smaller
just see if you can stay your *real* size
otherwise it ends up a tussle
of higher/lower, master/slave, winner/loser

you can't hide anymore

who you are is obvious to everyone
if not entirely to yourself
like the elephant trying to hide
behind a palm tree

THE ESSENTIAL NATURE OF THINGS

the essential nature of all things
is silence
the well we all drink from

the conduit for water
runs through everything
and changes into the pulse of electricity
from firefly
to lightning intermixed
with thunder

all of which is silence
moving

deliberate as glaciers
water creeps
in inches across the earth

I'D LIKE TO KNOW

what happens when
the soul is contained
in the container the body
and it bursts out into light
when it grows too big
to be held?

what happens
when sorrow soaks through
until it's way too deep
and the body floats away
so the soul seeps into clouds for its light?

what happens
when the body converts
then reconverts itself more
until we are all just dew
lying on the leaves for the sun?

NOT WHAT IT SEEMS

is everything a symbol
for everything else?

or is there a point at which
something is what it actually is?

these thoughts circulate
like gulls circling for food

it was only in this year
I noticed how far the surface of the ocean
dips and drops

the surface can't be trusted to be flat at all
its color should have told me
someone should have told me
but like so much of life
I looked but never knew

CARING

when it is new
caring has such a thin shell
vulnerable to the slightest pressures
tender to the touch
hey, everybody, don't drop it … it's an egg!

how hardy are you I'm tempted to ask myself
wondering how tough it could be
but I set aside such thoughts
of egg fractures
and Humpty Dumpty
and how all the king's men couldn't put him
together again

and instead I allow myself
to see kindness
and hardiness
and eggs
that keep their balance
on top of such
walls

ON THE WAY TO REAL

on the way to real
I keep falling

but aren't you supposed to be ascending?

in their practice
Buddhists blow themselves away
through particles of sand
in the mandalas
they build
then dissolve

but what goes in its place?

place is what I'm longing for
what it is mine
without battle

I look up at a blank sky

on the way to real
nothing is the is-ness
and everything is the none-ness

can the heart
just Geiger counter me there?

COMPANIONS

our emails open up
like the first scene in an epic novel
the vistas as detailed as
densely packed holy days

or like The Godfather
in the wide-shot wedding scene

we are quiet at times too
like a 2am recording
of Lou Reed
playing in a near empty diner

we are all these things

as well as
The Secret Garden
with its curling vines
and neglected rose trellises

or on some days like the tattered book binding
of an Arthur Rackham illustrated text
with women dressed in gilded gowns
with Rapunzel-like hair
accompanied by ladies in waiting

our electronic messages
lift off the page
in aerial twists and turns throughout the universe
the blue lights
on the keyboard
as atmospheric as those on airport runways
but we choose not to land
preferring to remain in air space
witty and free
unreformed
delirious in the pure ether
of thought word image transmission and speed

SOMEONE TOLD ME

someone told me pieces of our selves get fractured
and the angels start looking for them
hunting the four corners of the world
to return them to us

their wingspans serve reconnaissance duty

hovering over the dark places
reaching down between twisted girders
formed by natural or unnatural disasters
and grasp to find the remains of us

each sliver they find precious
a reverse holy shrapnel
that they clean and reassemble

placing it back under wherever it belongs
or releasing it to a nevermore

we breathe more deeply then
restored by this benevolence

and recognition of our selves returns--

loved and lifted
we are raised above the writhing
the divine restored to our human forms

ABOUT THE AUTHOR

Pianta is a poet, fiction writer, and editor whose work has appeared in journals such as *Nimrod International Journal*, *Adirondack Review*, *Ekphrasis*, *Terrain.org*, and *Bamboo Ridge Press*. Originally from O'ahu, she has lived in California and North Carolina but has returned to the Big Island in Hawai'i. Her readings often incorporate music and other media. Her website can be found at www.pianta.org.

RELEASES
More info about books, music, and editing at:
www.pianta.org

FICTION
Old Volcano Road
A woman struggles between physical and spiritual worlds
to save the life of her brother
Contempory novella set on the Big Island of Hawai'i
eBook and print versions
Kindle and Amazon

MUSIC
Little Bird: Songs for Children
Album of original acoustic children's songs
Available on iTunes, Amazon, Apple Music
Listen to samples at **https://pianta.hearnow.com/**

POETRY
Hawai'i Poems: from there to here
A capturing of the senses in contemporary Hawai'i
Amazon.com

We Don't Know What We Don't Know
For the times when it's unclear if we're floating or falling
Amazon.com

All Ends Never Ends
Love and music and their inexplicable ties
Amazon.com

The Secret of the Stem
Chapbook
Poetry, Prose, Fiction Excerpt
Celestials, fairies and what is real and magical
Amazon.com

Before
Chapbook
Micro-collection of poems on distance and the heart
Amazon.com

A Man in Parts
Chapbook
An 8-part poem about a mechanic who drops everything
for a new life in Italy
Amazon.com

Acts and Intentions
Chapbook
Personal and political events and the undercurrents
within them
Amazon.com

SHORT FICTION
Floating
Chapbook
Whimsical story about love and a mysterious
event in a small town
Amazon.com

Note: Chapbooks are smaller collections on select themes..

www.ingramcontent.com/pod-product-compliance
Lightning Source LLC
Chambersburg PA
CBHW071845020426
42331CB00007B/1858